# <u>Kosmish</u>
## and the Horned Ones

## Z.M Wise

Kosmish and the Horned Ones
Z.M. Wise

© 2018 Z.M. Wise
Cover image from 123rf.com

Weasel Press
Manvel, TX
www.weaselpress.com

ISBN-13: 978-1-948712-30-9

Printed in the U.S.A.

# TABLE OF CONTENTS

*To Kosmish...you know who you are. You, my friend, are the living embodiment of the arts in a perpetual state of sweetest chaos intermingling with love. To this day, you inspire and dazzle me.*

*To my dear ally, the Goat: here is to five years of your wisdom, wit, and never-ending code of ethics. May you and your twin flame prosper in this dimly lit planet and every planet beyond..*

# Characters of Kosmish and the Horned Ones

- **The Ram:** A creature of little self esteem, he desires and loves Kosmish more than anything or anyone. His determination shows as his highest characteristic.
- **Kosmish:** Also known as the 'Kosmish Lady' or 'Fox-Like Swan,' this mystical being gradually captured the Ram's heart. She is a giver, a polyglot, and creator, revered without being called a goddess.
- **The Wolf:** For quite a while, Kosmish has felt that her heart belongs to this humble and modest animal. The Ram wants to prove them both wrong, even if the endeavor ends up turning out to be completely hopeless.
- **The Lamb:** A wanderer of loneliness, a timorous creature who cannot stand the thought of someone competing for love.
- **The Goat:** The Ram's best friend, she is a wise and spiritual animal who shares a similar situation, but with a man of music. He is not her soul mate, but her twin flame.
- **Pan and Baphomet:** Minor contradictory creatures of myth, seldom proof that good can triumph over evil.

# Kosmish & The Horned Ones

## I – The Horned

Fare away,
far away,
sailed past the seven charted waters
and found not one face.

The Sacred stay here.
The Horned stay here.

Buffalo: extinction by arrows,
weaponry made without an effortless trace.
The bulls have charged to death.
The addax and ibex have said nothing,
but when do they ever speak?
Gazelle and antelope have
made themselves food for
arrogant idols.

Dragons have flown into volcanoes,
swallowed by Hawaiian gods.
Why breathe fire when we can
give it to the last dying race?
The moose,
withdrawn from all elk.

The oxen have lost their touch.
The yaks have retreated to the East.
Being holy with the Vietnamese ocean
serve as higher functions than other quadruped beasts.

They all search for that unicorn,
the One who Breaks the Forces.
Other realms see her as a deity,
and the graves fill with the soil of remorse.

Narwhals swim peacefully in spite of endangerment.
They worry not of tides turning.
But, their time was finite, their century falls under.
A new presence glides this way, daydreams burning.

Now leaves one goat to rule the Mystic Mountain,
one Lamb to stand in between it all,
and the Ram who fell for a shadow of a lady.

*October 4, 2016*

## II – The Fall of Baphomet & the Rise of Pan

Triple-Horned demon,
son of unholy water,
father to the masses,
born from the stomach of a
sacrificial mercy girl.

You burst forth like a crocodile from international
waters,
shocking the followers.
Rampage begins when it means to.

"How I love the women!
Tender hearts numb the pain and
stick between the teeth.
How I tower over you, anyway!"

No objectification but the object of consumption.
A satisfied demon is an elated demon.

"How I love the men!
Tough as the homes they mold from ground clay,
but tougher between the teeth.
How I tower over you, anyway!"

No manipulation but the conning of a meal.
A demon's stomach is proud to be full.

"How I love the children!
Innocence comes and innocence goes,
but the blood flow is as pure as day!
How I am infatuated with the quantity of bites!"

Swallowing a child of purity causes a
fire to surround his throat.

Baphomet dissipates and every human turns to artifice.

Gluttons for punishment gather in the
greenest of native forests to hear
Him play,
a satyr from the world of making.
One charm and all anthropomorphic dreams come true.

He plays not the lyre,
for the strings are a tedious mess.
He plays not the harp,
for the melody would be an uneven shambles.
He pounds not on hollow rocks,
for his hands would bleed out of vanity.
He blows not the Ram's horn,
for the religious ears would be scarred.

Oh, pan flute,
Oh, pan flute,
let us hear sequential notes!
Oh, pan flute,
oh, pan flute,
sing songs of the demonic entities that were smote!

Imperial empire of glorious behavior,
the masses are temporarily cured!
Let them hear the music that
lost itself in the Years before Unity.
Half man,
half goat,
but all smiles of pleasure!
Join in the company of dancing dusk.

*October 2, 2016*

## III – Ram (The Ram)

Never asked for love.
It was brought to me by the
golden boughs of the Sun.
Never pursued the thought of love.
My heart is medieval armor,
clanking awfully close and weighing four tons.

Spontaneous as the four seasons,
as playful as a wildcard.
A warrior as much as a statue,
as talented as a novice bard.

"Never go seeking love,"
the mystic sheep would say.
What do they know, other than the Eldest Ways?
"If you find it, guard yourself until the end."
Endless words,
out of the beaks of the most senile birds.

The grass tastes lovely today,
a mundane, ho-hum experience.
When can we expect a solidarity storm?
A little excitement for the sake of convenience!

The Horns of Penalty weigh me down,
yet the journey leads to the conclusion.
If life has been clear from the beginning,
why have I felt decades of confusion?

It's the Ram of the land.
Confidence level: next to nothing.
What does it matter if he is dealt the shortest hand?

Never dreamed of love,

for it belongs in fables and allegories
from the books underground.
Never spoke of love,
for the mere mention of it was considered slander.
Since the Days of Now, society never made a sound.

The cavalry of one has arrived,
defending the internal organ that will never be taken.
Glorious changes in the works,
a statement ultimately mistaken.

What is this I see,
cacao bean eyes of an emerald glow,
with no added presence to show?
Spotted me behind the trees,
laughing up to brand new heights,
expanding my unsightly sight?

A being so gentle from afar,
the wildlife, trusting her to no end.
How could her heart be that colossal?
She gives me the look as she would give a friend.

A letdown of proportions untold,
but I could not let fate decide.
I will prove my worth, sacrifice it all,
forgotten regrets being cast aside.

Now the Ram of the damned,
bitten by the pinkish aura of love.
Will he accept her offering hand?

*October 4, 2016*

## IV – Jewels Enter Nirvana: A Poem for Kosmish

It was you in that art gallery
in a fogbank dream.
It was you who I looked upon.

It was you in the bed of curiosities,
lying there, listening to Coltrane.
It was you who I saw,
raven-haired, multicultural beauty,
mind of orgasmic happenings.

Waited many moons,
many eons of mystic gatherings,
to glimpse at your goddess face and figure,
to wade in the river of your thoughts.

Songs set aflame near the lake of
esoteric folk singers, despising the studio and
living in the lap of luxurious company.

Your words are historic documents
found in the primeval mandala sands.
Your art and musical gifts of extension:
visions for the blind and
operatic symphonies for the deaf.

I am your grateful silhouette,
the one who kisses your fingertips
and caresses the nerves,
massaging the worries and simmering them.

And we exchange mutual glances.
And we have each other passionately.
And we kiss and make new constellation myths.

Separation is a boulder,
a boulder balancing on a bindle.
A grave for your loss and
yet another chapter of your life begins.

Envy is a killer of silence,
but, oh, the Canterbury heir
seems grand in the homely abode.

See others as they see you:
the living embodiment of a
jewel entering nirvana.

You are the gem in a
human rock pile, shouting,
"Syd is the reason for life!
Equality is the eternal ruler!
Poverty, no more! Your problems come first!"

Your grand organ of a heart,
the actual Eighth Wonder of the World.

The naysayers have seen nothing yet.
Grotesque canvas creations: the true beauty.
Your smile speaks determination, hidden by unnecessary doubts

I am a satyr,
a pan flute-playing admirer of yours,
as lowly as the forest soil,
but higher than the clouds for you!

And we synchronize brainwaves.
And we touch and intertwine fingers.
And we sing praises to living spirits in the dead of night.

*September 26, 2016*

## V – Wolf

Senses not diminished,
mind as sharp as the
teeth I use for defense purposes only.
Alone, I reside on the English side of the forest.

The Horned Ones never did any harm,
so why attack out of necessary necessity?

Surviving and thriving as an herbivore,
I desire no taste for meat.
They age, the agile bones needed for
disasters headed for the inner rim.

They call me 'Wolf,' but I
claim Protector of All that is Pure.

Come and seek my counsel,
for I live to serve with words and
spread the joy of living!

Why won't the Lamb speak to me?
What does he sense?
Why does the Goat turn her back to me?
What does she sense?
Why does the Ram possess a green aura?
What has he to be envious of?

Oh, but what connection is this?
Far beyond anything I deserve or fathom.
Initiation is biting down.
Patience is biting its tongue,
bleeding profusely as a crimson star.
Dare I approach her?

Even a Canis deserves
a smidgeon of happiness.

Her presence makes the fur rise
and reverts to black from the
grey of time in memoriam.

Oh, courage, help me say the
right set of words.

Do I detect another being,
someone who wishes to confess
his undying love?
He questions it and succumbs to
low self esteem.

His downfall is my miracle of a chance,
my blade of whistling grass.

Running through untold woods,
letting my paws rub against softness.

I have found life yet again,
for she fills that meaning!
Never before has my spirit been so cleansed.
Never before have I seen the
bodies ignite such sparks.
I have purpose!
I have fulfillment!

Wolf, the domineering predator,
softer than the soil.
"Let me imprint you, dearest creature.
Let us live out the end of years."

*October 4, 2016*

# VI – The Goat

Lonesome, the morning doves never fail.
All those cult kids of red will be back tonight.
They sacrificed my parents and
stoned my brother, but they will never want me.
Never for the virgin skull,
they will never want me.

They call me Warlock of the Field,
summoning pestilence with my vocals.
A con artist, I am not, for the
suspicions stem from the raving locals.

A lovely breed, I claim to be.
The males in the herd want no one else.
And though the males want no one else,
not one will initiate a dialogue with me.

The Ram knows who I desire.
We are destined to be twins of flame.
He knows not of my existence,
for the fires will call out his name.

Sheep cheer me on.
Pan plays encouragement songs.
The Ram says it is sudden fate.
Baphomet merely laughs and says I am quite wrong.

I come from the mountain.
I enter the meadow with
hair as white as ocean foam.
Meditation and peace of mind, oh distractive mellow.
The hour of the Twin Flame is nearly home.

*October 2, 2016*

## VII – Kosmish Lady Blues

Twice seen with the art of the macabre,
once in her sacred den.
Twice seen with the art of the macabre,
once in her sacred den.
Although the heart has been robbed,
the light of the self speaks through Zen.

She has the hair of midnight and one,
astrology in her eyes.
Her mind tells the tales of lore.
There is too much reality to fantasize.

She has the voice of long-awaited reason,
heart of white gold immaculate.
Her manifestations make the planet revolve,
but true love has won the gambling bet.

Insignificant Ram,
limping with the case of the Kosmish Lady Blues.
English Wolfen beat him to confession...primordial
news.
His tears of defeat are how he paid his dues.
Best give the rest to distant Brother Lamb.

He covers his ears to evade the howling.
She turns to look, but only sees an ally.
Could there be a Styx River drop of a chance?
The words have been hibernating.
Awaken them from a slumber in vain.
Confess before the Earth Child and take your stance.

Those blessed Kosmish Lady Blues,
those damned Kosmish Lady Blues...

The condition is the Kosmish Lady Blues,

lifts the spirits high.
They call it the Kosmish Lady Blues
and it will lift the spirits high.
After a time of feeling low,
why not dip our astral bodies in the purest skies?

Biology of beauty,
a revered appearance like no other.
To meditate with her would be a privilege,
a giver, a polyglot, a dream in color, a lover.

Thinking straight is no longer an option,
for her centralized image is breathtaking.
Photographers weep and citizens bow.
The gestures of selflessness: the unthinkable in
peacemaking.

English Wolfen imprinted on her first,
leaving the disoriented Ram an outcast among sheep.
They bleat and scream, but they feel the urge to weep.
Why think about defeat when seductive fingers lead to
sleep?
Counting the fence-jumping siblings…better than
quenching an empty thirst.

She has never parted the sea without
thinking of the wildlife first.
So many faces look up to her to complete the task.
He's never been afraid of the truth until now.
Why compare one's self to destiny?
So, why wear a Ram skin and Wolf's mask?

Those blessed Kosmish Lady Blues,
those damned Kosmish Lady Blues…
can we belong and exist as one?

*October 4, 2016*

## VIII – The Lamb

I look in the mirror and
the mirror breaks.
Cracks in the glass,
ugliness in the shards of one too many mistakes.

Falling into that other portal,
I see a silhouette of myself.
This is who I am.
No longer the Spirit Wolf of the evening,
no longer the master maker of my parchment's domain.
Vulnerability: the name, the moniker of the Lamb.

Lightning on either side,
crashing down on confessional booths.
Write it out and speak, now.
Do tell what massacres you committed in your youth.

Sacrificial blood, placed on every door.
No ethereal hands will touch the first born of this house.
Spirit Avenger of the Empire!
Families live to see another day.
Children yearn for another night of sand.
And the elders look for the next queen to sire.

Songs sung in the padded room,
cause and effect lead to sudden doom.
Catastrophic, torrential uproar!
For once, the Lamb guides us to the shore.

Just a little Lamb,
grazing in the grass.
Legs shaking, knees buckling, salvage me.

I turn to the shepherd,

but the shepherd hands me the staff.
An empty field before my eyes,
irony takes the shape of a distant laugh.

Tales of new reached the readership
of a thousand cult leaders.
The followers never gave a damn.
Paths not taken sell countries by the currency.
Troglodytes kiss their own image,
because no self-righteous human cares for a Lamb.

I've seen every tragedy known to us.
Homicides planned the dead pretending.
Never the better, the counter protestors
holding the cardboard of the cause they're defending.

Riding the dragon to the underworld region,
climbing the side of the Norse mountain,
singing a secular humanistic psalm.
Reading the poetries of the deceased,
spouting the oral words of Greek fire,
eating the futuristic fortune lines out of her palm.

Just when conformity laid itself to rest,
a haunting dream awoke the Head Seer.
Building upon reflections,
see the look of guilt through that same broken mirror.

Just a little Lamb,
bleating in the meadow.
Legs shaking, knees buckling, let me taste the final hope.

*September 28, 2016*

## IX – Ram and Goat

Crossing streams of lapped water,
I feel a sense of strength.
I will proclaim love to the
spiritual siren, the mirage maiden.
She is as authentic as these crimson cheeks.
Thoughts of her race back and forth.
But, the Wolf,
the unknowing moon mammal,
who she longs for desperately.
Who am I to try and divide destiny?
One word of selfish tongue and chaos could ensue.
For once, I care not.

I am all-knowing,
mystical, hoping for the prophetic union.
But, what about the chapter of my time?!
The flame is dying out and not
once has he looked towards the cliff,
noticing my trail of footprint evidence.
I know his music well.
It soothes me and cleanses my heart.
The tears will not cease.
I need a newfound mind,
a stranger preferred over a friend.
Give me grief no longer and let the
inferno burn me to a crisp,
for I love him!
I love him and not all the religion on Earth can stop this declaration

*October 2, 2016*

# X – Lamb

Make her come to you fully vigorous.
Make her be the muse of the night.

It is mental masturbation that
makes the draft, but the
ebony spurt of purity is liquid night delight.

Mistress, Master,
toes touch, candle maker.
Hooves tickle the grass and
in turn, blossoming laughter.

Separate distance from reality.
Make her come to you, fully vibrant.

*September 28, 2016*

## XI – The Ram and the Fortunate Wolf

I knew your mind the
minute the shepherd let me
loose upon this chaotic abyss.

You delicate swan,
you fox of faith,
I see you.
I heard your mind, racing with the
mensch-like thoughts of a monarch.

The mere fact that anyone dared to
talk down to you made these horns of mine
sharper than all the intelligence they could muster.

You delicate fox,
you swan of faith,
I memorized your body,
pieces of astrology.

You are the brightest star of all,
the outcast of a twentieth century.
How I loved it when you stood out,
for blending in is sickness incarnate.

I ignored the warnings,
for a hoofed being's heart can withstand anything.

Thunder of change,
sound of artificial waterfalls.
Vanilla amber scents,
constant smiles and laughter.

Oh, tears, I summon you, now.
Then, the howling began.

Why, oh why, did I miss that
tell-tale minute?
The Wolf found you first and the
mutual imprinting began.

Dropping the same tome,
listening to that catchy tune...
He may howl musical tones of melodic magic,
but do my a capella voice notes not count?

He may counsel the abused and disheveled,
but do my services for animals and advisement
mean absolutely nothing?

He may have held the signs,
but activism comes in many forms.

I curse you...
not you, Canis Lupis,
but your impeccable timing.

How I would gush such
words of fondness to the
fox-like swan, the swan-like fox.

She already mourns for the
severance of ties between her and the Other.

I curse you,
not myself, Stubborn Ram,
but the intentions of a selfish greed creature.

This beating organ has not been stolen
in a great duration,
so why must it happen when the
triangle between the Ram, Wolf, and Time
only becomes more self-evident?

Wolf, I beg of you,
let me borrow an ounce of respect,
for the Kosmish Lady deserves that and
palaces more.

She taught you the way as she
did so with me.

Admiring her from afar was not enough.
I needed every puzzle part,
every speck of sand grain,
and even then the thought without her was unbearable.

I did not ask for weeping sessions at
the mere thought of her smile.
It moves the plateaus of mountains
as it did so with my heart.

Damn you, heart,
covered with padlocks,
covered with chains,
covered with armor,
covered with cage bars,
surrounded by walls,
surrounded by barriers...

Why must your breath of fresh air
occur now in the hour of misfortune?

She is a cocoon, waiting to be reborn.
When she does,
your opposable-thumbed paws will
be there to catch her, will they not?

Choking whilst composing the verse,
I may as well be a sniveling Lamb,

shaking without the proper coat of wool.

You have become the reason to remain,
for if a firm negative is spoken,
may the North take me swiftly
so that my now-obsidian head will not look back.

Oh, swan-like fox, fox-like swan,
you are the ideal mate, yet
no one in this realm of spiritual planes deserves you.

Wolves may possess teeth, but if they
sink into her, the Ram will
live up to his name.

Guarded by horns of biblical references.
Forget my existence ever crossed yours,
Forget these turbulent visions.

Breathing is now a luxury.
Silent moonrise,
tainted clouds of paint,
add color to the sculpture of this manifestation.
The Wolf found you first.

A Ram, much too late for supper,
but isn't he always?

Rebuild the walls and barriers.
Cover the kisses with the chains and padlocks.
Cover affection over the armor and cage.
You bastard of a beast, wanting who you cannot have!
Blame the arrow of the flying cherubic shepherd,
letting me loose upon this chaotic abyss.

*October 1, 2016*

## XII – Goat Finds Her Twin Flame and Loves Him

Separation from storms,
purging from the absence of him...

Why must my clairaudient abilities
be blocked by the nightmarish memories?

Who will hear my tears on this mountain?!
Who will reassure my voice's stammer?!
Who will say sweet nothings to me?

The Ram is facing the trial of love.
And here I sit, confronting the cliff.
Its jagged point gives me clarity.

I *do* believe in second chances!
I *do* believe in the messages beyond the
river's tree trunk age-old ripples.

My horns,
stained from the backfire of
weeping in the wind.

O' Spirit Guidance,
keep me in suspense no longer!
Keep me in close proximity to the one
I want the most!

I can practically smell his musk,
the soulful chattering of his anxious teeth.

We would collaborate on the
growth of this matter called life.
We would make aesthetics a living being,
a diamond in the rough.

Pounding in the distance…
my eager heart?
His heart of internal battles?

Oh, from three trees away,
I can taste contact!

There, he sits!
Pleasant gentleman with a beard of
war stories and eyes of pain songs.

There, he pounds on Pan's hollow rock,
the one he never claimed.
"Call me a drummer,
the percussionist of confession."

Humanmade instrument, made for
instrumentation of humanity,
the scraps of bipeds.

They call us a blessed union of souls,
but the pending reunion held so much more.
From womb to tomb,
we have been cocoons!
The pupa bursts open and
reincarnation kisses the lips of one another.

Oh, these tears will be preserved,
marks of morbid history.

A dreamer can make it.
We walk with existential tiptoes.

Fair is the air,
now play me a love song of unity.

*October 4, 2016*

## XIII – Eventuality I: The Ram Triumphs and the Lamb Rises

Success of the times!
Revolver head spins as recklessly
as time's passing phases!

By the goddesses, the
Kosmish One chose *him*!
This is what a miracle feels like!

'Twas not the media-induced nightmares
that were imagined during the
Limbo of Fourteen Days!

How the needle of the clock's hand
crept ever so stealthily!
A bargaining chip: his heart of chains.
They broke free!

The Eternal Battle has laughed and forfeited!
Cup of water runneth over, but
dripped into the Lake of Ringing Bells.

A lapping of liquid reward,
rejuvenating for the senses.
Since he met her, he gained the sixth.

Happy go-lucky Lamb,
cheering him on whilst the
trampoline grass gives way for merriment.

On the planet of Earth,
all things knowledgeable will
rise above the meek, but the meek shrug off the temptation.
The Ram and raven-haired maiden are one.
The Lamb is a beast of bliss.

*Oct. 4, 2016*

## XIV – Eventuality II: The Wolf Triumphs and the Lamb Slaughters Itself

Aye, woe is the Ram who
cannot absorb the rejection that
he was expecting all along.
The psychedelic flowers told him so.
The screaming Sun told him to prepare.

Aye, Wolf Master needs no pack
now that he kisses her heart repeatedly.
Why must the two of them torture and
taunt the hoofed devil grasper,
the numb-hearted mammal?

To the North, he crawls,
through howling snow and such
turbulent seas, anxious to swallow him whole.

One last word from the Lamb.
"This Wolf would never consume me, anyway,
so what destiny must I look forward to?
To the madness of industrial farming!
To the slaughterhouse of rust!
There will be machines to guide us!
One frozen hook for me and
put yours next to mine."

Never a better time to take a
permanent leave of absence!

All he wanted was unified love,
but look at her, smiling at a new life.
Leave her be, stubborn ignoramus of love.
This life begins and ends with the self.

*October 4, 2016*

## OTHER TITLES BY AUTHOR

*Take Me Back Kingswood, Clock!*
*The Wandering Poet*
*Wolf: An Epic and Other Poems*
*Cuentos de Amor*

# About the Author

ZM. Wise is a proud Illinois native from Chicago, poet, essayist, co-editor and poetry activist, writing since his first steps as a child. He is co-owner and co-editor of Transcendent Zero Press, an independent publishing house for poetry that produces an international quarterly journal known as Harbinger Asylum. He has published four full length books of poetry, including: 'Take Me Back, Kingswood Clock!' (MavLit Press), 'The Wandering Poet' (Transcendent Zero Press), 'Wolf: An Epic & Other Poems' (Weasel Press), and 'Cuentos de Amor' (Red Ferret Press). Other than these four books, his poems and essays have been published in various journals, magazines, and anthologies, such as Feminine Collective, Occulum, The Unrest, Maudlin House, Camel Saloon, and Boston Poetry Review. Besides poetry and other forms of writing, his other passions/interests include professional voice acting, singing/lyricism/songwriting, playing a few instruments, fitness, and reading.

## Other Titles from Weasel Press

## Coming Soon from Weasel Press

*La Comadreja* by Sarah Frances Moran
*Young Thieves in a Growing Orchard* by Samuel E. Cole
*The Last Book You'll Ever Read* by Scott Hughes
*The Charred Axe Gospels* by Brian Kehinde
*Talk Like Jazz* by Joseph Cooper
*Requiem for the Plastic Clown* by Billie Duncan
Lipstick Stained Masculinity by Mason O'Hern
*Thirsty Earth* by Chris Wise